Loan Receipt

www.gflibrary.com

Jong, Erica. : Love comes first :poems
/Erica Jong. [006623497]

Due Date	Barcode	Call Number
11/25/2015	33108005276037	811.54 J732

Sincerely,

Circulation Department

LOVE COMES FIRST

ALSO BY ERICA JONG

POETRY

Fruits & Vegetables

Half-Lives

Loveroot

At the Edge of the Body

Ordinary Miracles

Becoming Light:
Poems New and Selected

FICTION

Fear of Flying

How to Save Your Own Life

Fanny: Being the True History of the
Adventures of Fanny Hackabout-Jones

Megan's Book of Divorce;
Megan's Two Houses

Parachutes & Kisses

Serenissima: A Novel of Venice
(republished as Shylock's Daughter)

Any Woman's Blues

Inventing Memory

Sappho's Leap

NONFICTION

Witches

The Devil at Large:
Erica Jong on Henry Miller

Fear of Fifty

What Do Women Want?
Reflections on a Century
of Change

Seducing the Demon:
Writing for My Life

Love

Comes First

· · · *Poems* · · ·

ERICA JONG

Jeremy P. Tarcher/Penguin

a member of Penguin Group (USA) Inc.

New York

JEREMY P. TARCHER/PENGUIN
Published by the Penguin Group
Penguin Group (USA) Inc., 375 Hudson Street, New York, New York 10014, USA ·
Penguin Group (Canada), 90 Eglinton Avenue East, Suite 700, Toronto, Ontario M4P 2Y3, Canada
(a division of Pearson Canada Inc.) · Penguin Books Ltd, 80 Strand, London WC2R 0RL, England ·
Penguin Ireland, 25 St Stephen's Green, Dublin 2, Ireland (a division of Penguin Books Ltd) ·
Penguin Group (Australia), 250 Camberwell Road, Camberwell, Victoria 3124, Australia (a division
of Pearson Australia Group Pty Ltd) · Penguin Books India Pvt Ltd, 11 Community Centre,
Panchsheel Park, New Delhi—110 017, India · Penguin Group (NZ), 67 Apollo Drive, Rosedale,
North Shore 0632, New Zealand (a division of Pearson New Zealand Ltd) · Penguin Books
(South Africa) (Pty) Ltd, 24 Sturdee Avenue, Rosebank, Johannesburg 2196, South Africa

Penguin Books Ltd, Registered Offices: 80 Strand, London WC2R 0RL, England

Most Tarcher/Penguin books are available at special quantity discounts for bulk purchase for
sales promotions, premiums, fund-raising, and educational needs. Special books or book
excerpts also can be created to fit specific needs. For details, write Penguin Group (USA) Inc.
Special Markets, 375 Hudson Street, New York, NY 10014.

Library of Congress Cataloging-in-Publication Data

Jong, Erica.
    Love comes first: poems / by Erica Jong.
      p.   cm.
    ISBN 978-1-58542-684-3
    I. Title.
    PS3560.O56L58   2009   2008042190
    811'.54—dc22

Printed in the United States of America
10   9   8   7   6   5   4   3   2   1

Book design by Meighan Cavanaugh

For Max, Darwin, and Beatrice,
Time's arrows

Contents

I. You Are There

II. PEOPLE WHO CAN'T SLEEP

III. APHRODITE'S LAUGHTER

Love comes first.

It matters the most at its worst.

—STEPHEN SONDHEIM

I.

YOU ARE THERE

HOLDING ON TO THE LIGHT

I plant my heart in the earth.
I water it with light.
The sweet, green tentacles
of Spring urge toward the light.
They nudge the earth like fat worms wriggling,
loosening light in the darkness.

They open the channels and passages
that allow the flow of life.

Sweetness follows them.
The sweetness of the new peapod,
the gingko leaf in May,
the sticky buds of the weeping cherry
not yet burst,
the fuzz of the pussy willow
in the pink hour
before dawn,
the small green arrows of the crocus
pushing through a glaze
of bluish snow.

. . .

Oh, light that nourishes life—
let us be mirrors
of your splendor.
Let us reflect your pure energy—
not dampen it.
Let us be givers of the light.

The dull earth turns
on its rusty axis.
The dolorous echoes of the dying
fill the ears of God—

who responds by planting
hearts with light,
hearts in the moving earth.

Let us learn to imitate
this infinite making of new hearts.

Air, water, earth are all we need.
and the miracle of the heart
alive with light.

The Poetry Cat

Sometimes the poem
doesn't want to come;
it hides from the poet
like a playful cat
who has run
under the house
and lurks among slugs,
roots, and spiders' eyes—
left so long out of the sun
that it is dank
with the breath of the Troll King.

Sometimes the poem
darts away
like a coy lover
afraid of being possessed,
feeling too much,
losing his essential
loneliness—
which he calls
freedom.

. . .

Sometimes the poem
can't requite
the poet's passion.

The poem is a dance
between poet and poem,
but sometimes the poem
just won't dance
and lurks on the sidelines
tapping its feet—
iambs, trochees—

out of step with the music
of your mariachi band.

If the poem won't come,
I say: Sneak up on it.
Pretend you don't care.
Sit in your chair
reading Shakespeare, Neruda, Sappho,

essential Emily
and let yourself flow
into their music.

. . .

Go to the kitchen
and start peeling onions
for homemade *sugo*.

Before you know it,
the poem will be crying
for love
as your ripe tomatoes
bubble away
with inspiration.

When the whole house is filled
with the tender tomato aroma,
start kneading the pasta.

As you rock
over the damp, sensuous dough,
making it bend to your will,
as you make love to this manna
of flour and water,
the poem will get hungry
and come
just like a cat
coming home
when you least
expect her.

Rapture

Two hawks live
on my hill.
I can tell
where the thermals are
by the way
they skim the sky.

They are scavenging
small creatures
but their flight
suggests rapture
to my upward eye.

CONTINENTAL DIVIDE

for G.S.B. of blessed memory

Handcuffed by time
I travel across this broad
beautiful America—
mesas, deserts,
peaks with clouds caught
upon them,
the Continental Divide,
where a drop of rain
must decide
whether to roll east or west

like all of us.

I speak to a group
of avid aging Californians
about daring to embrace
the second half of life.

The passions of the old
are deeper

than any wells
the young can plumb.

Meanwhile, you are dying
in a New York hospital—
your beautiful face drained
of blood
your arms too heavy
to seize the day,
your shining eyes
dimmed by pain
and drugs to dull it.

You have boycotted food,
yet all you can do is apologize
to your grieving children
for the trouble you cause
by dying.

"Don't worry, I'm fine,"
you say, eternal mother.

Solitary as you will ever be,
our love cannot save you
from this last loneliness,
this last rocky sea voyage
where no one dresses for dinner.

. . .

Meanwhile
I am listening to a doctor
who claims we can all live
to be a hundred,
a hundred and twenty,
if only we expand
our arteries with exercise,
our genitals with sex,
our brains with crossword puzzles,
poems, and proverbs.

Wingless, we can fly
over death
if only the body
—that laggard—
consents.

I suppose that drop of rain decided
to roll west with the setting sun,
taking you along.
The Californian doctor is quoting
Victor Hugo now:
The eyes of the young show flame,
the eyes of the old, light.

More light, Doctor!
How can we accept
time's jagged jaws
even as we are being eaten?

How can we endure
the extinguishing of eyes—
those mirroring all of mortality?

Doctor—
is death the aberration—
or is life?

As for love—
why is it never enough
to save us?

YOU ARE THERE

You are there.
You have always been
there.
Even when you thought
you were climbing
you had already arrived.
Even when you were
breathing hard,
you were at rest.
Even then it was clear
you were there.

Not in our nature
to know what
is journey and what
arrival.
Even if we knew
we would not admit.
Even if we lived
we would think

we were just
germinating.

To live is to be
uncertain.
Certainty comes
at the end.

IN VITRO

My zygotes
(once or twice
removed)
are frightened
of their
petri bassinet.

Who will be
sacrificed
and who spared?

Now that we can gauge
their genetic flaws
we pause
and contemplate
their fate.
God- or goddesslike
we break
their small
potential hearts in two.
Mitochondria to woo

perfection
in a stew
of DNA.

We never knew
such terrible
selection,
perfection,
resurrection
when we were . . .
(oh, were we ever?)

young.

Waiting for Angels

I do not know what to do,
my mind's in two.
—Sappho

Like Sappho,
my mind
is divided
between tribute
to angels
and dark hosannas—
to daemons.

I sit shiva
for the dead world—
where the bride's
hair is cut
to undo
her power
(everywhere but
in her home),

. . .

where a glass is crushed
to denote permanence,

where books
are looked forward to
like love letters,

where a rabbi,
priest, or shaman
may be asked
to define
good and evil.

And where we avidly debate
all night
about angels
dancing
on the filigreed heads
of silver—or golden—
pins.

No more.
All gone.

We celebrate our own
black masses in our beds
or on our blood-strewn streets.

. . .

We believe in no higher law,
no higher power,
no representative on earth
of the divine dialogue,
no one who speaks—
or even whispers—
eternal truth.

And so we wait
for angels,
hoping that these messengers—
half god, half human—
will fill the vacuum
of our hearts.

Never have so many
waited for so few!
Never has hope
had such sparse feathers
to fly upon!

In the dark air
of Armageddon
we hear the beating
of iridescent black reptilian wings.

. . .

Angels? Daemons?
How little we care
as long
as *someone*
comes!

Thank-you Note for a Grecian Urn

Heard melodies are sweet, but those unheard
Are sweeter; therefore, ye soft pipes, play on.
—John Keats

Three seated women
play three lyres
on the lekythos
you gave me.

They have been playing
for centuries—silent music
which reaches
only certain ears.

Their music has not yet
cracked the clay.

In the midst of the cacophony
of my demonic city,
I hear them singing—

about love, death, lust,
trust, betrayal—
all the old songs.

. . .

Their plucked strings
bring me back
to Sappho's island—
green as the mossy perpetuity
of poetry,
a well so deep
it does not echo
when you fall into it . . .

Sappho's island
is not like the other
burning isles of Greece.

It is green as that perpetual well,
shimmery with silver olive leaves,
round with golden grapes.

Its arms embrace
two deep bays
which seem like lakes
but mysteriously open
out to the sea
through narrow channels
like birth canals.

It is a female island
singing in the sea.

. . .

Some say the head of Orpheus
was washed up on its shores,
still singing,
after the Maenads tore him
limb from limb.

Legs dangling from the deck
of a borrowed sailboat
into the glaucous light
of the eastern Aegean,
I thought of you
and the love we share
for unheard music.

This lekythos once held
perfumed oil for a marriage
or a burial.
Does any drop remain?

We have been tuning
our lyre strings
for twenty years.
Shall we celebrate
before we mourn?

IN THE CLOUD FOREST

In the cloud forest
where the golden pumas leap,
flicking their rainbow tails
among emerald frogs
and verdant parrots with red combs,
the spirits of the Incas sleep
waiting to be born again.

They will appear in a world
without Spaniards, empty of conquistadors,
weaving their many-colored Quechua odes,
calling on mother earth and father sun,
to ripen their fat maize,
trickling clear water from the Andes
into a sacred music
unheard by European ears.

Without the wheel, without gunpowder,
innocent of smallpox, measles, plague,
what further wonders will they conjure?

. . .

Machu Picchu hovers between earth and sky
balanced on a ledge of cloud,
making tapestries of sunlight and solstice
in the pure, blue Andean air.

Who owns the future of the Incas?
Not Pizarro with his saddlebags of gold,
not Pachacuti the earth-mover,
not the military juntas of Peru.

The virgins of the moon
are waiting patiently to calibrate
the Inca future
on the high, green ledge
of their astronomical observatory.
They are waiting for the planets to align.
I am waiting, too.

Poem for a Fax Cover Sheet

Hating cameras, Plato said:
Look how everything grays
with duplication, blurs
at the edges. The Parthenon:
a postcard! And who are
those clowns loitering in
the (Kodacolor) agora?
Negatives of negatives?

AGAINST GRIEF

Sometimes we are asked
to carry
more than we can bear,
and the weight
is so heavy
that it seems easier
to lie under the earth
than to stride upon it,
easier to stretch out
in a damp grave
than to stand up
and salute the sun.

The past is a block of granite
suspended over your head
by a thin, gold wire
or a grand piano
floating up
to a ninth-story window
carrying all the chords
it has ever played,

or a portmanteau falling
from the old wire rack
of a long-distance train—
the Trans-Siberian Express
possibly—
or the rusty red train
that hoots
from Beijing
to Hong Kong,
carrying all the dreams

of the world's
most populous nation.

But the past
is only the past.
It takes
your present
to keep it alive.

The present is bright copper,
untarnished silver
slippery as moonbeams;
it is burnished gold.

It sings:

> *I am all the riches*
> *you will ever have.*

Afternoons in bed,
fresh raspberries
and cloudberries,
clear water
from a confluence
of mountain streams . . .

Catch me if you can!
Grab me!
I am a kiss, a caress,
a slice of yellow lemon,
a crystal tumbler of mineral water
studded with bubbles.
Drink me, Alice!

The chemistry
of the present
is volatile—
you must leap
into its test tube
with both bare feet
or it will turn
to base metal
and come back to earth.

There is time
enough for that.
Meanwhile, dance
on the bubbles

in your glass
as you were meant to.

Even a goddess cannot
grieve if she wants
to create new life.

I Dreamed That the Sea

I dreamed that the sea
had begun to swallow the land
and my old redwood hot tub
was full of dying shellfish—
crayfish missing claws, clams putrid
with death, opulent aphrodisiacal oysters.

You said: "The sea has washed up
unanswered questions."

But I live on a high rock ledge
miles above sea level.
If the sea reaches me here,
it will reach us all
and things submerged for eons
will die, gasping in their exoskeletons.

In my dream, I am building
an ark for these creatures—
and for myself—
though perhaps we are all past saving
even if we have such dreams.

FIGS

Italians know
how to call a fig
a fig: *fica.*
Mandolin-shaped fruit,
feminine as seeds,
amber or green
and bearing large leaves
to clothe our nakedness.

I believe it was
not an apple but a fig
Lucifer gave Eve,
knowing she would find
a fellow feeling
in this female fruit

and knowing also
that Adam would
lose himself
in the fig's fertile heart
whatever the price—

. . .

God's wrath, expulsion,
angry angels
pointing with swords
to a world of woe.

One bite into
a ripe fig
is worth worlds
and worlds and worlds
beyond the green
of Eden.

Risotto

The integrity of
the single grain of rice,
sun and water
fused in a starchy cup
to be filled up
with the essences
of our lives,
the rich brown broth
infused with saffron,
garlanded by
tidbits of porcini
more precious
than platinum
or gold.

I stand here
endlessly stirring
the ingredients of our lives,
watching the rice expand,
lose its translucency,
and become

a palimpsest
of fused flavors.

Oh, leftover life
in the sizzling skillet!
Stir, stir, stir
until you have concocted
that ecstatic paste,
harbinger of heaven,
manna of Milano—
risotto!

In Vino Veritas

I used to love it—
the first hit at the back of the neck.
The promise of love,
of poetry, of sex—
all in the chime and tinkle
of the mouth-blown glass.

What was I looking for
in those crystal depths?
Transport to
a realm
of pure spirit?
Transparency?
Transcendence?
It was never there.

But I remember
the dream.
Dear God, may
I find it again
with my own elixir.

Henry James in the Heart of the City

We have a small sculpture of Henry James
on our terrace in New York City. . . .

Nothing would surprise him.
The beast in the jungle was what he saw—
Edith Wharton's obfuscating older brother . . .

He fled the demons
of Manhattan
for fear they would devour
his inner ones
(the ones who wrote the books)
and silence the stifled screams
of his protagonists.

To Europe
like a wandering Jew—
WASP that he was—
but with the Jew's
outsider's hunger . . .

. . .

face pressed up
to the glass of sex,
refusing every passion
but the passion to write.
The words grew
more and more complex
and convoluted
until they utterly imprisoned him
in their fairy-tale brambles.

Language for me
is meant to be
a transparency,
clear water gleaming
under a covered bridge.
I love his spiritual sister
because she snatched clarity
from her murky history.

Tormented New Yorkers both,
but she journeyed
to the heart of light—
did he?

She took her friends on one last voyage,
through the isles of Greece

on a yacht chartered with her royalties—
a rich girl proud to be making her own money.

The light of the Middle Sea
was what she sought.
All denizens
of this demonic city caught
between pitch and black
long for the light.

But she found it
in a few of her books . . .
while Henry James
discovered
what he had probably
started with:
that beast, that jungle,
that solipsistic scream.

He did not join her
on that final cruise.
(He was on his own final cruise.)
Did he want to?
I would wager yes.

I look back with love and sorrow
at them both—
dear teachers—

but she shines like Miss Liberty
to Emma Lazarus' hordes,
while he gazes within,
always, at his own
impenetrable jungle.

FOR GRACE IN THE HOSPITAL

for Grace Darling Griffin, 1922–1998

The pink parasols
of the weeping cherry
remind me to give thanks
for another spring—
so unearned,
pure gift
we were never promised,
always given.

You, my friend,
caught between
letting go
and not letting go—
your body a shipwreck,
your soul a sail
hungering
for its big wind—
what shall I tell you?

. . .

That I need you here?
Selfish!
That you mothered
me and my words
with your abundance,
your Ceres-given gift
to make the earth blossom,
your amazing grace?

Grace, Grace, Grace,
what you have given me
can be passed on only
like mother's milk.
It is not intended
to be kept.

Weeping cherry
whipped by the wind,
I hold you flowering
in my heart.

Please stay.

SMOKE

The last time I got stoned,
turning the pages of memory as if they were a book,
I wrote with smoke
in the margins of my life
knowing that the future and past
are all one
and that the moment NOW is all we ever have.
Looking for lovers on the blink rims of our eyes
writing with smoke on the ceilings of our lives,
a paisley curtain that never stops moving,
a neon sign that never stops blinking—
mind expanding into eternity
with or without us.
Oh, smoke—
that we are and will become—
let me follow your spirals to the light,
leaving my body behind,
leaving my mind.

II.

PEOPLE WHO CAN'T SLEEP

THE GOD OF THE CHIMNEYS

What are the Jews after all? A people that
can't sleep and let nobody else sleep.
—ISAAC BASHEVIS SINGER, *The Family Moskat*

For what angry God
arching backward over the world,
his anus spitting
fire, the fetid breath of his mouth
propelling blood-colored clouds,
his navel full of burnt pitch and singed feathers,
have we given our eyes, our teeth,
our eyeglasses, bales of our hair,
and the magic of our worthless gold?

For what angry God
who tested Job,
and Abraham,
Moses, Esther,
Judith with the severed head of Holofernes—
for what atonement do we walk
again and again
into the ovens?

. . .

Invited with our industry,
our instruments—
bookbinding, goldhammering,
silversmithing—
given a ghetto, gold stars, curfews,
after some centuries,
we burst its seams
with our children and riches.
Then we are invited
into the ovens to die,
leaving our gold molars behind.

Who are the Jews after all—
but a people without whom
we would have to confront
the void in our own echoing hearts?

The symbol of our phoenix yearning
to rise
on the ashes of death?

People of the dream,
moving through history's
insomnia,
people who can't sleep.

WHEN JEW KILLS JEW

What does it mean
when Jew kills Jew,
when the old enmity
of Cain and Abel,
Judas and Jesus,
erupts again
in the city
of sepulcher and wall,
of women keening
for the loss of sons—
as Mary did,
and Eve before her?

When Jewish sons
forge prayer shawls into swords,
are drunk with the fumes
of gunpowder,
does God
flood Noah again,
unmake the dove,
the rainbow,

the parting of the Red Sea,
the deliverance from Egypt,
smash the tablets
and cancel
the covenant itself?

What shall we do
without commandments
emblazoned in living rock,
without prophets trembling
on Sinai?

Without the law,
without our brothers,
what is a Jew
but a convert
hiding from
the light?

When Jews adopt jihad,
the Inquisition reigns
and Hitler becomes
the new Messiah.

Then God sends us
impotent angels
who can only sing
falsetto
and are deaf

to the music
of eternity.

All this has happened
many times before.
The Diaspora's singing instruments—
auto-da-fé, poetry, prayer—
go mute.

And there is no difference
between walking
into the ovens of your enemy
and killing your own brother.

When Jew kills Jew,
God vanishes again
for another long sabbatical.

Firing thunderbolts with Zeus and Thor,
raping Europa for a lark,
playing amid the Bacchae
and drunken fauns,
God has no time for the people
he so carelessly created.

We walk out of the garden
barefoot, with uncovered heads.

. . .

God is not dead
but missing in action,
and we are destined to wander again
for more millennia
than there are undiscovered stars.

SLEEP

I love to go to sleep,
when bed takes me like a lover
wrapping my limbs in
cool linen, soothing
the fretfulness
of day glaring like
the Cyclops' eye
in a forehead
of furrows.

But I wake
always reluctantly, brushing
the dreamcrumbs
from my lids,
walking sideways underwater
like a crab,
spilling coffee,
knocking the mug
to the floor,
where it shatters
in a muddy river

to my continuo of
"Shit, shit, shit!"

What if death
is only a forgetting
to wake in the morning,
a dream that goes on
into other corridors,
other chambers
draped with other silks,
libraries of unwritten books
whose kaleidoscopic pages
can be read
only by the pineal eye,
music that can be heard only
by the seventh sense
or the eighth or ninth,
until we possess
an infinity of senses—
none of them
dependent on flesh?

What if our love of sleep
is only a foretaste
of the bliss that awaits us
when we do not have to wake again?

What frightens us so
about falling?

To drop the body and fly
should be as natural
as drifting into a dream—
but we are insomniacs
tossing on soaked sheets,
hanging on
to our intricate pain—
while God with her sweet
Mona Lisa smile
sings lullabies
the ears of the living
cannot hear.

Sentient

Awake at four
with the old brain beating
its fast tattoo—
I want, I want—
I think of love,
of the hot scramble
of limbs in darkness;

of the mind
pulsing its secrets
in metaphor;
of synapses firing
need, longing, love;
of the body
with its midnight hungers;

of the mind
caught between dream and waking,
wondering what it is,
self-creating always;

. . .

of God,
whatever she is
asking the questions:
Who are you anyway,
and how did you get here,
and what is the distance
between two stars,
between two brain cells,
between two lovers?

Here in the rosy
pink-ringed dark
all the birds
are sentient in their own way
as we—
on the verge
of wakefulness
and song.

PRAYER TO KEEP BACK THE DARK

November and the sun
grows sparse in the sky.
The last fly perches
on the white nose of Punchinella
made by my Venetian mask-maker,
Massaro,
who is dying.

Soon the bare birches
will be clad in ice,
and squirrels will steal seed
from the birds'
swinging larder.

The deer will tiptoe
in search of sweet green leaves
and find none.
The wild turkeys
will fly, fly
away from Thanksgiving.

. . .

The earth is God's book
but in our blindness,
we have obliterated letters
so we may say
God has abandoned us.

It is we
who are illiterate.

Unable to read
the runes of divinity
around us,
in love with the idea
of being orphans,
we write to bring back
the dead.

Elephanta

To spend your whole life
carving one plane
of Shiva's face,
to shape stone
in the dark,
leaving no signature
but your passion
to make godhead
manifest,
this these monks knew—
and we have lost.

Go into the cave
of yourself and see
if you can touch
the Braille of your being—
a pinch of dust thrown
in eternity's eye
which does not even
blink.

Speaking with the Dead

Speaking with the dead,
I try to hear them
instead of my perpetual monologue.

What have you learned?
I ask.
And they reply:
That we are leaves in a storm,
salt dissolved in the sea,
that a year reduces us
to our irreducible elements
which are speechless in the old way
but full of the sound
an earthworm makes, burrowing,
or a bird falling out of the sky.

No—don't mourn for us in this new form
which admits no mourning.
Mourn for yourselves
and your unlived lives,
still full of questions.

. . .

Language, while you possess it,
can heal you.
Take this salve, this balm,
this unguent
with our blessings of silence.

COLLECTING VENETIAN GLASS

Because it is fragile,
because it is full of light,
because its gold threads
are nonnegotiable
except to the seeking eye,
because it is a basket
that holds only delight,
because its cup runs over
then shatters forever,
because we see ourselves in it.

In Venice, clever craftsmen wrought
these harbingers of human fate:
luminous,
friable,
mortal—
therefore I collect them.

These wine goblets and flower bowls
will self-destruct,

molten silica
becoming glittering dust.

Will my descendants puzzle over
these fragments of my life?
Will they wonder
what they held
when they were whole?

Broken glass can tell
as much as anything—
shards of pottery,
centaurs without legs,
Pegasus grounded wingless,
Aphrodite stripped
of her Archaic smile,
wearing only breasts, belly, sex.
Sappho's lyrics scrawled
on ripped papyri—
these bits speak history's
tattered tale.

How we cling to
scraps,
shards,
sea glass—
because we cannot stay.

BEAUTY BARE

for Angelo Bucarelli

> *Euclid alone has looked on Beauty bare.*
> —EDNA ST. VINCENT MILLAY

> *Helen being chosen found life flat and dull*
> *And later had much trouble from a fool.*
> —WILLIAM BUTLER YEATS

We are not in Troy
but still a man
with three daughters
may have much trouble
from fools
and a woman who bears
three daughters is a heroine
in my book
even though
I am not Homer—
and even though Homer
had little use for heroines, who were not witches.

. . .

Nina, Angelo,
this new beauty
you have made—
this beauty bare—
affirms life
in the midst of death—
affirms your Vita Nuova—
also mine.

The middle of three daughters,
the joker in the pack,
the meat in the sandwich,
I know the gravity
of what you've done.

For what fairy-tale king and queen
do not have
three daughters?
And what are daughters for
but to drag their parents
kicking and screaming
out of fairyland?

But here comes Helena-Sirai
with her fierce desire to live,
her fists beating,
her tender feet kicking the air
until it eddies about her,
altering everything.

. . .

Suddenly Cosima becomes
the eldest of three Graces
painted by Botticelli,
Springtime's summoner,
ringleader of the muses.

And Palma becomes herself,
only more so—in the middle,
winning her place with wit.
(Sometimes the one
whose place is least assured
strives hardest to be heard.)

What will the world be like
when these three do their dance?
May we be there
to witness it!

A glow of Eden suffuses
your three blond beauties.
Oh, may they return us to
the Golden Age—
Cosima, Palma, Sirai—
may they dance us back
on their thirty pink toes
to the garden we left
so long ago.

III.

Aphrodite's
Laughter

Talking to Aphrodite

I. THE PRIESTESS ATTEMPTS TO RETIRE

Aphrodite, I have toiled
in your service forty years
and I am still alive to tell it.

Those I have loved—bandy-legged smiths
and lost boys,
defrocked shamans in the night,
warlocks of the left,
doctors who could not heal themselves,
poets whose lives did not scan,
gigolos tangoing on tossed bedsheets—
I have mostly forgotten,
but your service I have never regretted:
it has brought me
all the wisdom I have earned.

Once a woman came to me in your likeness—
eyes blue as the sea on a sunless day,

skin pink as the dawn
rising over my Connecticut ridge
at four when I awaken to your worship.
I knew her as your stand-in
and loved her as if she were
myself in a mirror—
all for love of you.

But now I want to quit
this worship,
give up my priestess' robes of red,
my gold chokers, my silver bells, my black pearls,
and go naked into simplicity
becoming poetry's crone,
a white witch of rhyme,
a tree-hugging pagan philosopher,
grandmother to my daughter's
new, green passions.

But you—joker Aphrodite—
send me another man
to worry my pulse
and fill my eyes with mischief,
my skin with false dawn.
What is another man
but trouble?

. . .

Sappho, being fifty and past mothering
her precious Kleis,
loved a ferryman
who ferried her to the cliff
from which she jumped—
or so the story says.

(But what could Ovid and Menander
know about the heat of a poet's heart
tangled in a woman's breast?)

Take away this Phaon!
This agate-eyed aging Adonis
wooing me with words!

But even as I say this
your most secret eyes meet mine:

"Just one more tumble into ecstasy,"
you tease. "Who knows what hymns to my glory
you will write now,
at the peak of your powers?

What are the lives of poets
but offerings to the goddess they adore?
Do you think such worship is a choice?
Even immortals
obey her capricious laws."

II. BLOOD OF ADONIS

In April, when the blood
of Adonis blooms
on every slope above
the Mediterranean,
my blood blooms too.

You do not love like that
without exsanguination.

Even Aphrodite bleeds
where the great tusked boar
gored her love.

But she remains alive
forever to her pain—
the curse of goddesses.

Adonis sleeps.
Lethe is the milk
of mortals.

III. APHRODITE EXPLAINS

Some say Phaon
was no ordinary ferryman

but a daemon
who plied the glittering waters
between Lesbos and the mainland.

One day I arrived
in the guise of an old woman:
hairs sprouting from my chin,
collapsed jaw, a few brown reeking teeth,
sad dugs with nipples pointing earthward,
feet yellowed with calluses,
an Aeolian lyre with broken strings
in my brown-dappled hands.

But Phaon greeted me
as if I were a girl of twenty.
His bright eyes revived me,
made me young again.

Asking only a kiss
he ferried me safely back to Lesbos.
And for his pains
I gave him the fabled alabaster box
filled with the magic unguent
that makes women love.

Phaon could have his pick
of young buds.
If he loved Sappho,
he loved her truly,

. . .

not for her youth
but for her poetry and prescience.

But Sappho was
a mistress of imagined slights
like all you self-singers.

And when he rowed in late,
his muscled arms gleaming,
his ferry decked with flowers,
she cursed me, daughter of Zeus,
for a fabricator of falsehoods,
and cursed him for deceit,
pelting his cheeks
with fiery menopausal tears.

She imagined maidens her daughter's age
spread upon his bed of sea-borne flowers—
and leapt to her death
from the Leucadian cliff
simply to spite him.

I am Aphrodite
and I sail the skies
in a golden chariot
drawn by swans
that beat the air into submission

with their wings.
I see the past and what is yet to come
and I can bend the hearts of men
to passion if I choose.

But here my power stops:
I cannot save a singer
seduced by her own song.

IV. WHEN?

When do we give up love?
My daughter begins her adventures
with that cock who crows so insistently
morning, night, high noon,
and neither I nor Aphrodite
can undo its upstanding magic
with moon-dew at its tip.

But I am wise
if not yet quite old,
wanting the poem
more than the lover,
wanting words
more than the sticky dew
men secrete in their
private places.

. . .

I teeter on the edge
of love—deciding whether or not
to give the body sway.
My hormones are not hot;
my blood boils
only for poetry or power.
My black trance of night
does not need a man to fill it.
And you, golden Aphrodite,
with your swans,
mean more to me as muse
than as harbinger of love.
The rose-ankled Graces
will dance for my pen
even if I dance alone.

"Not so fast, Priestess,"
you admonish me.

"Would Orpheus have sung
so sweetly
had Eurydice come home
from Hades on her own?
Would Persephone still be
'the Maiden whose name must not be spoken'
if she spent all the year
picking daisies with Demeter?

Would Pygmalion have made Galatea
so beautiful without
that last deep debt to me?

Heifers with gilded horns,
snowy goats with silvered horns
stampeded through the streets
on my feast day,
and maidens burned incense
of vanilla and myrrh,
strewed petals of the rarest Lydian roses—
blue and lavender—
and still I did not bless
every lover unrequited
on bended knee.

I give my favors sparsely, if at all.
I give my favors only to the brave."

V. APHRODITE'S LAUGHTER

A sudden thunder
of swans' wings
and I am awake.
The sky is streaked
with ruby, tangerine, pimiento—
lavender banners
divide a molten core

of cumulus clouds—
and suddenly she is there
rolling across the heavens
in a chariot of burnished gold,
her crown of towers burning
like a city set ablaze
by incendiary armies,
her forehead a show of
scenes of the Trojan War.

My Lady, Aphrodite, Venus,
fairest of goddesses,
sticking one shell-colored toe
in the Aegean,
paddling long, thin fingers
in the Baltic,
your sex a great South Sea
of liquid pearl—
you cover the world
with your mischief,
making populations burgeon
beyond our poor earth's power
to bear.

You laugh, uncaring—
a goddess' laugh.
Hecate attends you
with her jet-black panthers,
her gleamless jewels of night.

Poets die to become
speaking instruments
to sing your praises.
Maidenheads fall
like hyacinths grown
too heavy to stand.
Purple stains streak the skies.

Too-persuasive goddess,
visit other planets for a while.
Earth has had enough
of your beneficence.

The scalloped foam at the edge
of the shore
is full of dying creatures,
lost limbs of crab,
turtles without shells,
oysters drying out
in crumbling sandcastles . . .

Go to the moon, Aphrodite,
and make it breed!
Go to Mars, your lover's
red planet, and raise
the Martian plankton
into spacemen and galactic women!

.   .   .

If anyone can do it,
you can!
But leave us alone
on earth
to catch our breath.

You laugh again,
putting a torch to my heart,
lifting your robe
above your rosy knees
and whispering, almost hissing:

"Death is
good enough for mortals,
not for gods.

The planets are my playthings
and their inhabitants my toys.
And who are you to question it?

Sappho, for her pains,
jumped off a cliff;
and Sylvia stuck her head in the oven,
leaving her mate to become Poet Laureate.
Anne wrapped herself in furs
and fell asleep forever,
leaving her daughters
to decipher
her coded messages.

. . .

But you want to be a poet and not die?"

Aphrodite's laughter shakes the sky.

VI. APHRODITE'S DAY

I have always loved Friday,
your day, my lady, the night
the week erupts into love . . .

Venerdì, says my small red
Italian calendar
perpetually rounding
off the days
as they tumble
one upon another
like worn pebbles
in a rushing stream,
as they blur into bitter blue,
round red, rushing gold.

Where do the days go—
each one irretrievable,
each one full of silver seconds,
moments of the purest fire.

. . .

Is life much too long
for an immortal?

Do you scan the skies
looking for trouble
because of the boredom
of being beautiful
forever?

Do you play with your people—
placing a Sappho
before a Phaon,
Sylvia and Ted
just so—
and wait for the disaster
you know must happen
to amuse you?

Life is very long
for gods and goddesses,
and mortals are their movies,
their entertainment centers,
their soap operas.

Is that what I am, to you—
a soap opera?

Perhaps even less.
I would like at least
to be a long novel
layered with subplots.

And so you play with my heart—
setting a fire in one ventricle,
a flood in another,
a hurricane in my blood—
"The touched heart madly stirs,"
as Sappho said . . .

Ah, Sappho's soap opera
reverberates down
through the centuries
touching even our own
antipoetic age.

Poets are pebbles in a stream
animated by your laughter.
Everything we do
is your proclamation.

A man looks at a woman
and she sets him above
the gods and heroes.
A woman looks at a man
and he sees her as Aphrodite.

.   .   .

You merely pass the time,
making millennia fly by.

You are the prow
of the ship called *Poetry*
and you smile
your antic smile
as the world explodes
in your father's skies,
making nebulae

for your name's sake,
amen.

Both here on earth
and in the heavens
every day is

Aphrodite's day.

VII. CONJURING HER

Mandarin oranges,
love apples,
honey in a jar,

last year's rose petals,
dried gardenia whose pungency
lingers in the air
and a shred of brown paper
burned at the edges
with his secret name upon it
in heavy grease pencil,
my name, too.

Love has ignited
the edges of my life
and the honey
saturates his name
at the bottom
of the round, clear jar—
a little womb of wishes.

I have kissed the lid,
lit incense sacred
to you, my lady,
and now I wait
for him to fill
my honey jar,
if it pleases you.

It pleased you to see
Arion rescued by his lyre,
clinging to it in the stormy sea
as if it were a dolphin's back.

. . .

It pleased you that Sappho's
fragmentary verses
went to make sarcophagi
for the sacred alligators of Egypt
and were saved
—a papier-mâché patchwork
quilt of poetry
spared by time.

Lady of papyri and sarcophagi,
lady of lovers' jumps,
lady of spells and incense,
of goats and heifers
bleating to the sacrifice,
of maidens and madonnas
silently doing the same,
I bow my head
to your unending miracles—
I surrender to your power.

Some say love is a disease,
a fire in the blood that burns
every human city down.
I'll take my chances.

Before I curl
like incense to the sky,

before I study how to die,
drizzle the honey
of my wishes
on my waiting tongue.
Teach me how to fly.

VIII. SAPPHO: A FOOTNOTE

A nightingale sang
at her birth,
the same nightingale
who sang
in Keats' garden.

She tried to hold
the sky in her two arms
and failed—
as poets always fail—
and yet the effort
of their reach
is all.

She understood
that her life
was the river
that opened into the sea
of her dying.

. . .

She understood
this river flowed
in words.

Her harp
buoyed her like Arion's
as she drifted toward
the all-forgiving sea.

Most of her words
vanished. Millennia
flew by.
The goddess she worshipped,
born of the sea's pale foam,
grew younger
and more beautiful
as the words of the poet
dissolved.
All this was foretold.

Sappho burned
and Christians burned
her words.
In the Egyptian desert,
bits of papyri
held notations
of her flaming heart.

. . .

Aphrodite smiles,
remembering Sappho's words:
"If death were good,
even the gods would die."

You who put your trust
in words when flesh decays,
know that even words
are swept away—
and what remains?

Aphrodite's smile—
the foam at her rosy feet
where the dying dolphins play.

IX. HER POWER

All around the crumbling
limestone shores
of the Mediterranean
there are traces
of her power—
the queen of Cythera,
foam-footed Aphrodite,
she who makes the muses

dance together,
plaiting poppies
in her golden hair . . .

Temples to her capriciousness
stand everywhere
facing the sea
which is full of nereids,
dolphins, blue and gold tiles
of sunlight, and caves where
the moon hides between pregnancies.

I have always been drawn
to these shores
as if I knew
the goddess I worshipped
would be found
looping the ancient isles
made of limestone,
most soluble of stones.

She took the moon on her tongue,
the silver wafer, tasting of lemon,
giving a lemony light.
She watched the waves erase
her filigreed footsteps.

. . .

She is everywhere and nowhere—
provoking love in the least
recess of longing.
She is the goddess for whom
the earth continues to spin—
in her turning
all endings end
and all beginnings
begin.

ELEGY FOR PEGASUS
(On the Death of Barbaro)

Swift knew about horses,
that they are
more rational than we,
that they stand
on their strong, slender legs
like a good argument,
that they are
beautiful in flight,
beautiful at rest,
beautiful of face and form,
that we grieve for them
as for our best selves,
that we love them
not as pets but as gods,
that when we race them
we are racing ourselves,
that none of our betting
and borrowing
can sully
their nobility.

. . .

They prance,
they fly
and we cannot.

Oh, winged horse
of poetry,
lift me
to the perfection
of Barbaro
with his fragile legs,
let me fly
through the clouds
on his back—
racing to that
green meadow
where horses and humans
speak like equals.

About the Author

Erica Jong began her career as a poet long before she wrote her classic novel *Fear of Flying*. She is the author of twenty-one books of poetry, fiction, and nonfiction. Her books have been published all over the world.

231579520